Advanced Python

Adam Stewart

Table of Contents **Page**

Introduction

Getting started in coding can be complicated sometimes. You may worry that you won't be able to figure out what all of the symbols and words mean. You may take a look at some of the statements and feel like it is too hard to understand or that you will spend too much time to write the syntax before you can get anything started.

But when it comes to getting started with a coding language, one of the best ones that you can work with is Python. Python has been around for just a short amount of time, but it is based on the English language so it is easy for even a beginner to get started with. But if you have some experience with coding, you will love how powerful this tool is and how you will be able to combine together Python with some of the other coding languages to get everything done that you want.

This guidebook is meant for the more advanced user in Python. If you have had a chance to work in Python in the past, but want to be able to do some better things in your programming and get a fun program set up, this guidebook is going to help you out. We will spend some time talking about the different syntaxes that you can add to your tool belt in order to get some amazing code. Add some of these in with the huge library that comes with Python and you are going to be able to write any kind of code that you would like.

When you are ready to get started with writing in Python this guidebook is going to help you to make it to the next level. You are going to learn all of the great tips that you need to do some impressive things when writing out your code!

Chapter 1: Getting Started with Python

If you are someone who likes to work with computers or who has a great idea that others would be able to use to help make life easier and more, learning how to code can be one of the best choices that you make. It allows you to mess around with some of the different statements that are available and make games, have message come across the page, and so much more.

This is one of the easiest programs that you will be able to use. It has all the features that the more advanced user is going to love, but you will still be able to use and enjoy this system even when you are just getting started with Python.

While some people are scared about getting started with coding languages because they look too confusing to even get started with making your own, there are some fantastic programming languages that you will be able to use even as a beginner.

One of the best programs that you can use when you first want to get started with your very own code is Python. While this guidebook is going to work on some of the more advanced commands and other things that you can work on within this language, the Python program is good whether you are a beginner or you have been working in coding for years.

Python is considered one of the easiest coding languages to learn. It is simple to learn thanks to being based on the English language so you won't have to worry about learning new signs and symbols that don't make sense. It has the power needed to do some great programs and you will even be able to combine it with some of the other programming languages that you are interested in.

There are so many reasons why you would choose to go with Python over one of the other programming languages and it is really the best choice to go with as a beginner. Some of the reasons why you would choose to use Python include:

- Easy to read—since this is based off the English language, it is really easy for most people to read. It doesn't have a lot of crazy characters that you need to learn and you will be able to put in words that you know.
- Clean—other programs use a lot of symbols, brackets, and other things in order to talk to their compiler and

get the code executed. This can make a big mess when you are first getting started in the code and you may have some issues reading through the whole thing. But with Python the code has fewer symbols around and it is fine to use indents and tabs to help the code look nice.

- Powerful—despite being so easy or even a beginner to get started with, Python has the added benefit of a lot of power. Those who have worked in coding for a long time will appreciate that this program will still give them some of the power that they are looking for.
- Works with other programs—if you are a fan of another programming language and want to try out Python, you will be happy to know that this coding language will work with others ones as well. Or if you need to complete a task that is not possible with just Python, you will be able to combine it with another option to get everything done.

It is easy to install Python onto your computer and it is going to work with a lot of the different computer systems that you are going to use. You will need to go online to find a way to download this, just make sure that you are installing the IDLE environment (this comes with Python when you download it), as well as the text interpreter (Notepad in Windows works well), can help you to get started on this and ensure that you are going to get the process to work in the right way.

Whether you are an old expert at using coding and you have been doing it for a long time or you are just getting started, Python is one of the best options for you. It is simple to use, has a lot of functionality, and you will be able to complete almost any task that you would like on this language.

Now that we have a little bit of an idea of why Python is such a great product to use and why you would want to consider using it in your coding language, let's take a look at some of the exciting things that you will be able to do when you decide to go with Python as your programming language.

Chapter 2: The Built In Functions Found in Python

When you are working in Python, there are a number of functions that are already going to be present for you to use. The interpreter is set up to already recognize these functions so as long as you put them into the code properly, Python is going to do a lot of the work for you.

There are quite a few of them so this can make things so much easier for you when you ae writing your code. Some of the functions that you will be able to use within your code when they are needed include:

- abs() This one is going to return the absolute value of the number. You can use a floating point number or a long or plain integer if you would like. If your argument is a complex number, this is going o return a magnitude instead.
- all() This one will return true if all of the elements in that statement are true or if it is empty.
- any() This one will return true if any of your elements are true, or if there are no elements.
- bin() this number is going to convert your integer number to a binary string. The result is going to be an expression that is valid in Python.
- bool() this one is going to return a Boolean value. This means that the answer has to be true or false. It can only be used in these kinds of instances.
- Bytearra() this one is going to return to you a new array of bytes.

- Classmethod—this one is going to look at the function that you place into the system and then give you a class method based off that.
- Cmp() this one is going to compare two different objects, such as x and y, and then will return to you an integer according to the right outcome.
- Compile() this is going to cause the objects in the statement to be executed or evaluated so that you can see the results.
- Complex() this is a class complex. You will be able to return a complex number to the real value or even convert a string or number over to a complex number. If the parameter is a string, the program will interpret it as the complex number and then the function needs to be called without having another parameter. The second parameter is not allowed to be a string.
- Dict()—this one is going to create a new dictionary. This can be helpful when you want to keep a few of the codes that you are working on in line without needing to rewrite them or do anything else.

- Eval()—this is when the expression argument is first parsed and then evaluated as an expression in Python. This will be done using the local and global dictionary in your namespace.
- Execfile()—this function will be similar to the exec statement, but it will parse a file rather than doing this to a string. It will also not use a module administration and it will read through the file no matter what while also not creating a new module.
- File()—you can use this in order to open up a file in the program, but it is often saved for testing rather than this other function. The best way to open a file with Python is to use the open() function.
- Filter()—you will first need to construct a list of elements that you would like to use. Then the filter will be able to go through this list and determine which ones are true and filter those out.
- Float() this is going to return a floating point number that was constructed from a string or number x.

- Format()—this is going to convert your value to a representation that is formatted. The interpretation of what is formatted will often depend on the value argument that you use though there are some built-in formatting types that can be used.
- Id()—this is the identity of the object. This is the integer that is guaranteed that is unique and will remain constant for that particular object for its lifetime. If you have two objects that don't overlap with their lifetimes, they are able to share the same id() value.
- Input()—this function is going to be the input that you want to show up on the screen. It is not going to be used in order to catch errors on the user side. For example, if the input is not placed in properly, there is going to be a SyntaxError that is raised.
- Int()—this is going to give a return of an integer object constructed from a string or a number x or a return of 0 if there are no arguments given for this.

- List()—this is going to return a list which items are the same, as well as in the same order, as the original irterable's items.
- Locals()—this will update as well as return a dictionary representing the current symbol table. Free variables will be returned by this as well when it is called using the function block but not the class block.
- Long()—this will return a long integer objected.
- Map()—this will apply the function to every item on the iterable and will return a list with all of the results.
- Max()—this will return the largest item that is inside of the iterable or show you the largest of two or more arguments.
- Min()—this one works in kind of the opposite since it is going to return the smallest item in your iterable or at least the smallest of two or more arguments.
- Object()—this will return to you a new featureless object.
- Open()—this is the best way to open a file as well as return an object to the file type that you want. If there

is something wrong and your file is not able to open, you will see the IOError.

- Print()—this is one of the most common that you will see. It tells the interpreter to print the objects to the stream field. It is basically when you are telling the interpreter that you would like that string or statement to be printed on the screen.
- Range()—this is a really versatile function when it comes to making a list that will need arithmetic progressions and you will often see it in loops.
- Reduce()—this will apply the function of your two arguments going from left to right so that the iterable is just down to one value, even if there are more.
- Set()—this will return a new set object, sometimes with elements that have been taken from the iterable and it is one of the built-in classes.
- Str()—this is a string that will have a representation of the object placed inside and in a format that is easy to print.

- Sum() this is the function that will find the sum of the iterable going from left to right and then will return the total.
- Tuple()—this is going to return a tuple that has the items that are the same as well as in the same order at the iterable's items.
- Type()—this will take one argument and will return the type of an object. The return value will be the type object.
- Zip()—this function is going to return a list of tuples where the i-th tuple will contain the i-th element from each of your sequences. The new list is going to be truncated in length to a new length that is as long as the shortest argument sequence.

These are just some of the functions that you are going to be able to use in order to make the code work the way that you would like. Adding them in will tell the interpreter to behave in a certain way compared to others and can ensure that you are getting your program to work the way that you would like.

Keep in mind that there are many other functions that you are going to be able to use when you are in Python so mess around with a few and try them out in the interpreter to get the best results.

Take a look at this list any time that you want to try out something in particular with your code, or would just like to mess around a bit and see what everything does in the program, to see the results.

Chapter 3: Using File Input and File Output

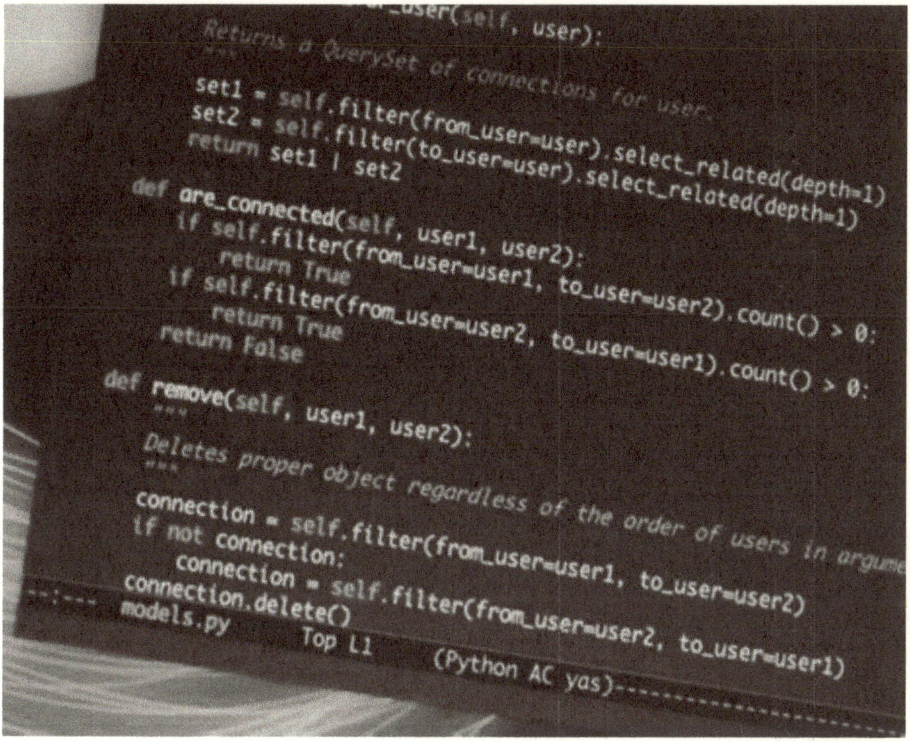

Next we are going to explore some of the things that you will need to do when trying to store the data in your code to use later. Sometimes you will want the data to last for a bit longer. It isn't practical to write out a code and then just use it once and everything is all done.

There are times when you will need to store your data in a way that you will be able to retrieve it later and even display it, either in whole or as a part, on the computer again. This is usually considered a “file” on a disk. Let’s take a look at how you are able to perform these operations when you are creating code with Python.

There are some different file operations that you are able to carry out when you are working on a Python file mode. Think of these kind of like saving your code like you would when using a Word document, but you are saving code instead. Some of the operations that you are able to carry out include:

- Creating a new file
- Closing a file
- Moving to a different location in the file; this is also known as seeking
- Writing to a file
- Opening and reading an existing file.

Let's take a look at how each of these are going to work when you want to deal with a file that you are working on in Python.

Create a new file

The first thing that you can do is to create a file. In order to write onto a file, you will need to open it and then choose the mode that you would like to write in. You have three choices when opening this file including the exclusive creation mode (x), append (a), and write(w). If you bring up a file that already exists and you want to use the (w) mode because it is going to allow you to make changes the best.

Any time that you would like to write a sequence of bytes or a string, such as when you are working in binary files, you will need to do the write() method. This method is going to return a number of characters that is written into the file and can make it easy to add in the changes that you would like in this program.

Let's take a look at what you are able to do with the write() function to help you make some changes to the content that you are writing.

```
#file handling operations
#writing to a new file hello.txt
f = open('hello.txt', 'w', encoding = 'utf-8')
f.write("Hello Python Developers!")
f.write("Welcome to Python World")
f.flush()
f.close()
```

With this file, you are creating everything in the current directory because we did not take time to specify where we want it to go. So the hello.txt file is going to be located din the current directory. When you open up the file, the message that you are going to see is "Hello Python Developers! Welcome to Python World."

Now it is possible to overwrite that same program and get something that is a bit different. Let's take a look at how this would work when you want to add or change something to your program with the following syntax.

```
#file handling operations
#writing to a new file hello.txt
f = open('hello.txt', 'w', encoding = 'utf-8')
f.write("Hello Python Developers!")
f.write("Welcome to Python World")
mylist = ["Apple", "Orange", "Banana"]
#writelines() is used to write multiple lines in to the file
f.write(mylist)
f.flush()
f.close()
```

After you save this file, the message that you will get when it comes up on the screen will be "Hello Python Developers! Welcome to Python World Apple Orange Banana."

You can also make some changes that allow you to append the message that you write. This is going to work in slightly different ways. For example, if we added the 'a" after the file name of hello.txt, we would have a different kind of return show up. It will allow you to add in a few more lists if you would like, add in more statements, and even more.

Creating a Binary File

When you want to write out your data as a binary file, you will need to write them ore as a sound or an image file. You can even change some of your normal text data into a binary file, you just need to make sure that you are supplying the data in an object form so that you can expose the data as bites. A good example of using this would be:

```
# write binary data to a file
# writing the file hello.dat write binary mode
F = open('hello.dat', 'wb')
# writing as byte strings
f.write(b"I am writing data in binary file!/n")
f.write(b"Let's write another list/n")
f.close()
```

Once you have this written out, you can open up the file using notepad to have an idea of what you just wrote onto the disk. You would need to use the encode or the decode function in order to read or write the text that you are getting from a binary mode file. An example of how to do this is below:

```
# write binary data to a file
# writing the file hello.dat write binary mode
f = open('hello.dat', 'wb')
```

```
text = “Hello World”

f.write(text.encode(‘utf-8’))

f.close()
```

Opening up one of your files

So far we have looked at some of the ways that you are able to create and then store some of the files that you want to create, but at times you may want to open up one of the files that you have been working on.

Let’s bring some of these back from the disk so that they can be read on your program. A good idea of this is as follows:

```
# read binary data to a file
#writing the file hello.dat write append binary mode

with open(“hello.dat”, ‘rb’) as f:
        data = f.read()
        text = data.decode(‘utf-8’(
```

print(text)

the output that you would get form putting this into the system would be like the following:

Hello world!

This is a demo using with

This file contains three lines

Hello world

This is a demo using with

This file contains three lines.

Of course, when you want to read through a file that has some kind of text on it, you should take the time to open it in text mode.

Seeking in a file

There are times when you will want to move around some of the things that are in your file. You may notice that there is something that does not match up that well or that you have misspelled a word in some place.

Changing the file position can help you to get into the right spot and find any location in the file that you would like. You simply need to tell the code that you would like to find a certain spot and then you can get there to make the changes that you would like.

You will be able to use this formula at any time to ensure that you are getting the file position right where you want it and if you use some of the syntaxes in this chapter, you will find that it is easier than ever to tell the system what you want it to do.

There are so many things that you are going to be able to do to your files based on how you want them to work. There will be times when you may need to pull the file back up for later or mess around and make some changes.

Python makes it easy to add in the changes that you need to keep the program running smooth and to easily find any of the information that you need along the way.

Chapter 4: Working with Regular Expressions

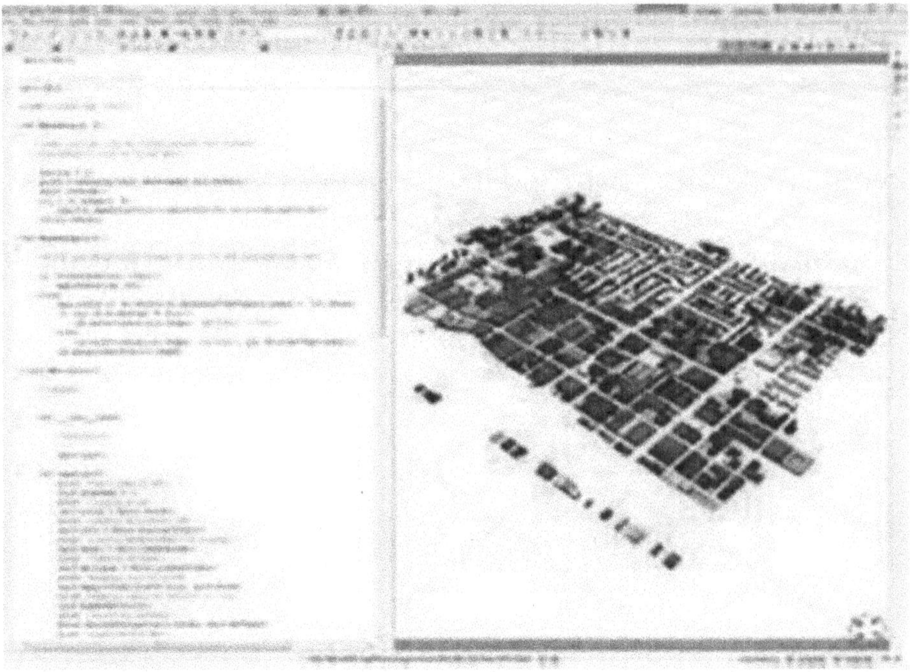

One of the neat things about working in Python is that it has a really powerful library. This library is known as regular expressions and it is responsible for handling many of your searches as well as extracting different tasks elegantly.

These expressions are going to be used in your language in order to filter our various texts or texstrings. It is possible to check and see if a text or string will match up with the regular expression.

The good news is that when it comes to working with regular expressions, you will use the same syntax with pretty much all of the script languages that you may choose to use.

This means that it is going to work and look the same as you would find with many other programming languages including Java, C#, C++ and more. Also, make sure to realize that sometimes regular expression is going to be written out as regexp or regex so if you see these you know what they mean.

So what are regular expressions and how would you use them. A good way to show how you can use a regular expression is to locate a word that has been spelled in two different ways within your text editor. We will show you some of the different things that you are able to do with the regular expressions to really make things look amazing.

There are many different ways that you ae able to use regular expressions in your coding and it is important to learn how to use these within the code to get it to do what you would like.

If you would like to use regular expressions, you must import the expression library through Python. You will need to do this at the beginning of the program so make sure that you bring it with you whenever you are downloading this project to ensure that everyone is going to be able to use the library if they are creating code in your system.

There are a variety of different expressions that you may choose to use in your statements and understanding how to get them to work and what all they can do will make a big difference in how your code is going to be executed.

Let's take a look at some of the regular expressions that you can choose to use in your code, what they are all able to do, and how you can make them work inside of your code.

Basic patterns

The great thing about regular expressions is that they are not just responsible for specifying fixed characters, they can also specify patterns if you would like. Some of the basic patterns that you are able to use in Python with these include:

1. a, X, 9, < -- ordinary characters just match themselves exactly. The meta-characters that aren't going to match themselves simply because they have a special meaning include: . ^ $ * ? { [] and more.
2. . (the period)—this is going to match any single except the new line symbol of '\n'
3. 3. \w—this is the lowercase w that is going to match the "word" character. This can be a letter, a digit, or an underbar. Keep in mind that this is the mnemonic and that it is going to match a single word character rather than the whole word.
4. \b—this is the boundary between a non-word and a word.

5. \s—this is going to match a single white space character including the form, form, tab, return, newline, and even space. If you do \S, you are talking about any character that is not a white space.
6. ^ = start, $ = end—these are going to match to the end or the start of your string.
7. \t, \n, \r—these are going to stand for tab, newline, and return
8. \d—this is the decimal digit for all numbers between 0 and 9. Some of the older regex utilities will not support this so be careful when using it
9. \ --this is going to inhibit how special the character is. If you use this if you are uncertain about whether the character has some special meaning or not to ensure that it is treated just like another character.

Performing a query with the regular expressions

There are several methods that you are able to use when trying to perform a query on your input string inside of Python. The methods that you are able to use include:

- re.search()
- re.match()
- re.findall()

The search method

This method is going to be identified by the search() function and it will be able to match anywhere. The nice thing about the search() function is that it isn't going to restrict you to finding matches that are just at the beginning of the string.

It allows you to find things that are somewhere else within the string, such as at the end of the string, if this is how you would like the program to work. Let's look at how this is going to work when you are placing it into one of your syntaxes:

```
import re
string = 'apple, orange, mango, orange'
match = re.search(r'orange', string)
print(match.group(0))
```

The output that you are going to get from this is going to simply be "orange". One thing to keep in mind with the search() method is that it is simply going to find a match once. Your example above had two "orange" in it, but the search function is going to just find it once and then will stop looking.

So once it found the first "orange" it stopped searching and would not have found the second orange. In this kind of example, it would not matter how many "orange" you had in the equation, you would only get one result.

The match method

This is going to work a bit differently than the search function. It is going to find the matches only if they happen right at the start of your string that is being searched. So for example, it is going to look for a pattern of some kind that is inside of the syntax that you search.

Using the same example as above, you can see that there is a pattern with the word "orange" appearing in between all of the other words. But when you add in the re.match function into the formula instead of the re.search, your result will be none.

This is because orange is not the first part of the string. If you had the string say orange, apple, orange, mango, orange, the re.match method would be able to find it and would give this as the result. If the pattern is not right at the beginning of the string, it is not going to find the pattern that you would like.

You can have any pattern that you would like, but it needs to start out the statement if you would like to have it show up in the results.

The findall method

This one is another unique one. If you are looking to get the statement to release all of one particular word in the string, you will need to use the findall method. Using the example above, you could type in orange for the re.findall and the result that you would get is "orange" "orange.

This is because you have two of the orange word within the string. You can do this with any of the other words that are inside the string as well if you would like to mix it up, but it doesn't really matter how many of each word is in the string. You can have ten of the orange word in the string and the findall method will help you to find all of them.

Square brackets

There are times in your syntax that you are going to use the square brackets in order to indicate a certain set of characters. For example, if you write something out in the statement as [abc], it is going to be a match for a, but, or c. Other codes, such a \w and \s will work inside of the square brackets; the only exception is that the dot is just going to be a literal dot and you will not be able to find a match with it when you have it inside of the square brackets.

These are just some of the regular expressions that you may want to use inside of your code. There is so much that you are able to do with these and they can make things so much easier when you are working hard inside of your statement.

Try adding in a few of these inside of your own interpreter to get some practice and to see how all of them are going to work and make a difference inside of your codes. Over time you will get the hang of what you are doing and be able to use some of these regular expressions in Python to make some extraordinary codes.

Chapter 5: What is Exception Handling?

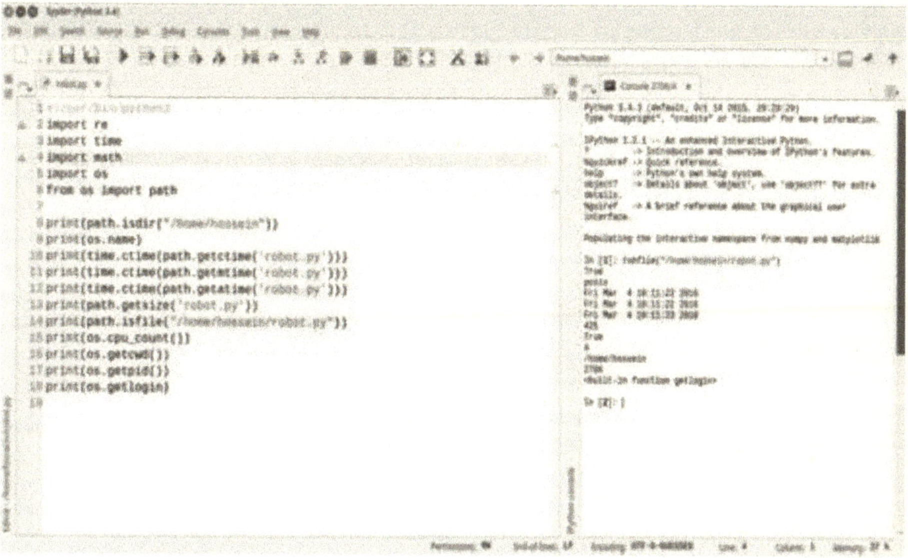

When you want to show that an abnormal condition has occurred in your coding, you will use an exception in Python. When a method comes across an abnormal condition, also known as an exception condition, that it isn't able to handle by itself, it may add in an exception to help it out.

There are a few exceptions that have been added into the Python library that will help you out with your code, such as one that is able to indicate when the conditions are going to read past the end of the file, or when you want to divide by zero.

It is possible to define some of your own expressions if you find that the Python library doesn't have the right information present or you want to do something a little bit different. In Python, you will see that an exception is going to be triggered on its own when it sees errors, and they can even be triggered and then intercepted in the code.

If you are interested in adding in an exception to your code, there are a few that Python will offer to you in your library. Some of the except handling statements that you are going to use in Python include:

- Try/except—this is when you will try and catch are used to try a block of code and then recover from exceptions raised by Python or by you.
- Raise—the raise will trigger an exception manually in your python code.

- Assert—the assert conditionally trigger an exception in your code.
- Finally—finally perform cleanup actions, whether the exceptions occur or not.

Raising an exception

If there is an issue that your code or the program is going to try and do something that is erroneous, Python is going to raise an exception to such conduct. An example may be something like this:

```
x = 10
y = 10
result = x/y #trying to divide by zero
print(result)
```

The output that you are going to get when you try to get the interpreter to go through this code would be:

```
>>>
Traceback (most recent call last):
    File "D: \Python34\tt.py", line 3, in <module>
    result = x/y
ZeroDivisionError: division by zero
>>>
```

Python is going to raise the error because you are trying to divide your number by zero and this is something that is not allowed when working with Python. It is possible to add in another part to this that will have a message come up, rather than the error message, to help you to show off that the user is not able to do this number. A good example of doing this is:

```
x = 10
y = 0
```

```
result = 0
try:
    result = x/y
    print(result)
except ZeroDivisionError:
    print("You are trying to divide by zero.")
```

This code is going to recognize that there is an issue with trying to divide by 0, but it is going to give you a message that will come up on the screen when this happens. For example, if your user does use this and try to divide by zero, you will find that the message "You are trying to divide by zero" will come up. You can change the message to something else if you would like depending on the situation. You can do this with anything that you will have an exception for to ensure that the user understands why the program is not working rather than just getting an error sign to show up.

Exceptions that are user defined

Sometimes when you are working on your code, you will need to raise up an exception that isn't against the coding rules in Python, but which meet a certain requirement for the program that you are trying to work with. It is not uncommon to custom create an exception class in this kind of program.

You will be able to create an exception class that will go with the rules that you want to set out for your program. For example, if you don't want someone to use a specific letter or number in the program, you can add in these exceptions. A good example of doing this may include:

```
class CustomException(Exception):
def_init_(self, value):
        self.parameter = value
def_str_(self):
        return repr(self.parameter)

try:
```

```
    raise CustomException("This is a CustomError!")
except CustomException as ex:
    print("Caught:", ex.parameter)
```

This is a great way to show a custom exception for your program even if it is not an exception in Python. When you use this syntax, you will get the message "Caught: This is a CustomError!" if the user puts in some data points that you do not want to have come up.

You will be able to set up your own customer errors to make them work with the results that you will allow within your syntax regardless of whether they are accepted by Python or you are just making your own rules at this time.

Exception classes are often defined by being able to do things that the other classes can do, but for the most part they are going to be kept simple with just a few attributes that will allow the information about your error to be extracted by the handlers for the exception. This basically means that you simply need to bring in the exception that you want the interpreter to recognize as well as the phrase or statements that you would like to come up when a user meets one of the exceptions.

If you want to create a module that will raise more than one error, the best practice is to create a base class for the exceptions that will be defined by that module and then go on to create a subclass that will work with the specific exception classes for different error conditions. This way the interpreter understands what you are considering exceptions from the beginning, you are able to make the classes that you want for just some of the exceptions if you would like to have in the syntax.

Defining the clean-up actions

There is another optional clause that you can use with the try statement. This one is known as the "finally" clause that is going to work to define any of the clean up actions that you want to have executed no matter the circumstance. A finally clause is always going to be executed before leaving the try statement, even if the exception never occurred. When the exception does occur though, and it is not handled by the except clause, it will be re-raised after your finally clause is executed. The finally clause can also be done on the way out when any of the other clauses in the statement is left via a return statement, continue, or a break.

A good example of how this is going to look when you write it into your code includes:

```
def divide(x, y):
        try:
        result = x/y
except ZeroDivisionError:
print("Division by zero!")

else:
        print("result is", result)
```

finally:

    print("Executing finally clause"

divide(2,0)

When you go through and execute this syntax, you will see the results:

```
>>>
Division by zero!
Executing finally clause
>>>
```

Working with exceptions is an important part of working in the Python program. There are some times when the language code is going to do the exceptions because it doesn't like what you are trying to do.

On the other hand, there are times when you will want to write out an exception that will only count when it comes to your program. You can work with the exceptions no matter the use that you want them for.

Exception handling can bring about some new and exciting things that you can work on within the program. Sometimes the program itself is going to have the exceptions and you will not need to create them. But depending on the program that you are working with, you may have to create some of your own to make the program go the way that you would like. This chapter will allow you to make these exceptions so that the program works the way that you want.

Chapter 6: What Can I do with Object Oriented Programming

As you are learning a bit more about the Python programming language, you may have heard about Object Oriented Programming or OOP. This is a special approach that is used for organizing and developing your program and it is designed in order to eliminate some of the pitfalls that come with using conventional programming methods.

It is going to do this by using the best structured program features and some new powerful concepts. It is a new way that you are able to make your programs and it can be used on many different languages.

Python is considered an OOP language which allows it to be easy to use without all the hassles and the bugs that you may find with some of your other programs that are harder to use. Let's take a look at how OOPs work and why you are going to love that Python has some of these features.

The Object Oriented Paradigm

Originally, many of the programming languages that were developed would use the procedural approach. This had many flaws inside of it that could make working in the code difficult.

This was the biggest motivating factor in developing OOP. OOP is going to treat data as an important element in how to develop a program and it does not let this data flow freely through the system. It is going to tie the data close to the function that will operate it and helps to protect the data from any accidental modifications from the outside function.

The OOP can do so many things within the function. It is going to be able to allow the decomposition of a problem into a number of entities that are known as objects and then will build the function and data in the objects.

The data of this object can be accessed by the function that is associated with this object and by nothing else. However, it is important to notice that the function of one object can sometimes access the function of other objects.

Some of the features that you are going to notice when you are using the object oriented programming include:

- An emphasis on the data rather than the procedure.
- Programs are going to be divided into objects.

- The data structures have been designed so that they will be characterized by their objects.
- The functions that operate with the data of a particular object are going to tie together inside the data structure.
- The data is going to be hidden and an external function is not able to access the data.
- The objects are able to communicate with each other through their functions.
- The new functions and data are able to be added if you would like to.
- Follows the bottom up approach when you design the program.

Basic concepts to know when working with OOP

There are a few different concepts that you can use when you are working on OOP. Some of the most common ones that you will need to know and understand when you are working in this language include:

- Classes
- Objects
- Inheritance
- Data encapsulation and abstraction
- Dynamic binding
- Polymorphism

Each of these are important parts of working with the OOP language and you are going to be able to do so much with it. Let's take a look at these different concepts within OOP that will help you to really build up your codes.

Classes

You can think of the classes within Python as the design or blue prints. The entire set of code and data for your object can be defined with the help of a class. In fact, the objects are variables of the type of class.

Once you have taken the time to define a class, you are able to create any number of objects that will belong within the class. Each object is going to be associated with a data type class that they were created in.

So basically the class is going to be a collection of objects that are similar in some way. They can have the same use, the same actions, the same colors, or something else you are able to define your class in any way that you would like.

For example, you could define a class about vehicles and then you are able to place in any kind of vehicle that you are going to be using inside of your program. Inside of Python, the classes are going to be user defined and they will often work just like built in types within the language.

Objects

Objects are going to be the basic entities to run time in the OOP system. They can represent a lot of different things such as a place, a person, a bank account, a table with some data, or any other item that you want to have the program to execute.

They can sometimes represent some other user defined content that you would like, including lists, time, and vectors. When you have a problem in your programming, it is going to be analyzed in the term of objects and how the objects are going to communicate with each other. Program objects need to be chosen carefully so that the different objects match closely with other real world objects as well.

Data encapsulation and abstraction

The wrapping up of data and a function into one single unit, also known as a class, is going to be known as encapsulation. This is one of the biggest and most striking features that you are going to see inside of a class. The data will not be accessible to the world outside and only the functions that are wrapped up into the same class will be able to access it.

These functions are going to provide a good interface for you to use between the object's program and the data. This kind of insulation of the data away from the direct access by the program is known as information hiding or data hiding.

On the other hand, the abstraction is going to refer to the act of representing some essential features without adding in the details or the explanation about its background. The classes will use this kind of abstraction and will be defined by different abstract attributes including cost, function, wait, and size.

They will encapsulate all of the different properties of the object that you want to create and sometimes they will be known as data members since they are able to hold information.

The functions that will operate on this kind of data can be called other names such as methods or even member functions.

Inheritance

When we are talking about inheritance in Python, we are talking about the process of which objects of one of your classes will acquire the properties of the object from another class. It is going to be able to support the concept of hierarchical classification.

The principal that comes with this kind of division is that each derived class is going to share some common characteristics from the class it is derived from.

When you are using the OOP, the concept of inheritance provides the idea that things can be reused. That means that you are able to add in some new and additional features to a class that is already in existence without having to modify it.

This is possible when you derive a new class from one that is already in existence. The new class is going to have features that were combined from both of the classes.

The real power and appeal in the inheritance is that it is going to allow the programmer to use one of the classes that they already made. You may not be able to do everything that you want with these, but it does enhance what you are able to do with the program and makes it easier to write some of the code that you really want.

Polymorphism

Next on the list is polymorphism. This is a Greek term which means having the ability to take on more than one form. In your program, you can have an operation that is able to exhibit different behavior in different instances. This kind of behavior is going to depend on the data types that you are using in your operation. For example, if you have a class that is a shape and it then has a draw method as well.

This can be nice if you need the object to do several things in the execution. You will be able to go with just one of your objects and turn it into a way to do many different things, helping to limit the amount of lines that you are using in your code and keeping things a bit more organized.

Dynamic binding

Another thing that you are able to do when you are working with an OOP language is dynamic binding. Binding is going to refer to the linking of a procedure call to the code to be execute din response to the call.

Dynamic binding on the other hand means that the code that is associated with your given procedure call is not known until you call it out at run time. It is sometimes associated with some of the other OOP features including inheritance and polymorphism.

A function call that is associated with a polymorphic reference will depend on the dynamic type that has been referenced. For example, if the inheritance brought about the draw method, every object is going to have this procedure. However, the algorithm is going to be unique to each of the objects so the draw procedure needs to be redefined in each of the classes that it is defining.

Python uses the OOP option in order to help you to make some amazing code without having to worry about all the mess and bugs that come with some of the older versions of codes. You will be able to combine together each of these different parts to help you to make some amazing code that will work in a great way when it is executed.

Chapter 7: Working on Objects and Classes in Your Python Programming

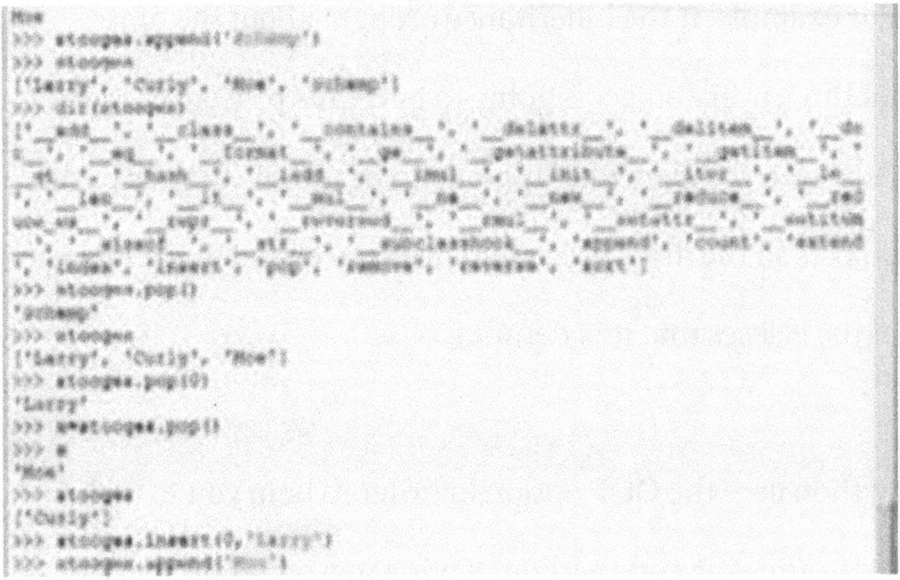

In the last chapter we spent some time working on classes and objects and seeing how they are going to work within your code. The classes allow you to place some different objects together so that it is easier than ever to pull them out when you execute your code.

The objects can be anything that you would like, but you should place similar ones into the same class to keep them all grouped together. With the right organization, you are going to be able to get your code in order and ensure that the interpreter is able to work the way that you want.

There are a few things that you should understand when you are getting started with using classes in Python including:

- Classes are basically the design or the blueprint for your objects and how the program will run.
- Creating objects using classes by instantiating objects.
- Objects that are inside the same class will have the same structures, but they can differ in some respects. For example, you can have a class named vehicle, but there are many different types of vehicles and they will vary.

Creating a class

Creating a class does not have to be complicated when you are working in Python. When you work on a class statement, you are creating a new class definition. The name of the class is going to follow right after the keyword class which is then followed by a superclass object that is inside of the parenthesis and is followed by the colon. An example of how you would be able to do this includes:

```
class Vehicle(object):
#constructor
def_init_(self, steering, wheels, clutch, breaks, gears):
self._steering = steering
self._wheels = wheels
self._clutch = clutch
self._breaks =breaks
self._gears = gears
#destructor
def_del_(self):
    print("This is destructor....")

#member functions or methods
def Display_Vehicle(self):
   print('Steering:', self._steering)
```

```
    print('Wheels:', self._wheels)
    print('Clutch:', self._clutch)
    print('Breaks:', self._breaks)
    print('Gears:', self._gears)
#instantiate a vehicle option
myGenericVehicle = Vehicle('Power Steering', 4, 'Super
Clutch', 'Disk Breaks', 5)

myGenericVehicle.Display_Vehicle()
```

The output that you are going to be able to get from putting all of this information into your interpreter includes:

```
('Steering:', 'Power Steering')
('Wheels:', 4)
('Clutch:'. 'Super Clutch')
('Breaks:', 'Disk Breaks')
('Gears:', 5)
```

This example is going to show a lot of the different things that you will need to make the syntax work. It is going to include the object definition, the methods definition, the attributes, the destructor function, constructor function, and class definition.

These definitions and uses will be discussed a bit more in the following sections so that you can learn why all of them are so important to helping you get the results that you are looking for.

Class definition as well as object instantiation

Both of these are important parts of the syntax that we talked about above. First, let's look at the different syntaxes that you will need to recognize in order to put these to good use.

Class definition syntax will be the following:

```
class subclass[(superclass0]:
        [attributes and methods]
```

The object instantiation syntax will look like the following

```
object = class()
```

When you want to invoke the methods and attributes within the syntax you will use the following options:

```
object.attribute
object.method()
```

Special attributes that can be used in Python

Outside of some of the self-defined class attributes that you are able to design on your own, there are some classes that will have special attributes. These can help you to get so much more done with your work and ensures that the interpreter has an idea of what you would like to get done with your syntax. Some of the special attributes that you need to understand with Python include:

__dict___ this is the dict variable of a class name space

__doc__ this is the document reference string of class

__name___ this will be the class name

__module__ this is the module name and consists of the class

__bases__ this is the tuple that will also contain all of the superclasses

Let's take a look at how this may work within one of the syntaxes that you may choose to work with.

```
class Cat(object):
    itsWeight = 0
    itsAge = 0
    itsName = “”
    defMeow(self):
    print(“Meow!”)

    defDisplayCat(self):
```

```
        print("I am a Cat Object, My name is", self.itsName)
        print("My age is", self.itsAge)
        print("My weight is", self.itsWeight)

frisky = Cat()
frisky.itsAge = 10
frisky.itsName = "Frisky"
frisky.DisplayCat()
frisky.Meow()
```

When you are using this as your syntax in the interpreter the result that you will get on the screen is:

```
('I am a Cat Object, My name is', 'Frisky')
('My age is', 10)
('My weight is', 0)
Meow!
```

Accessing the Members of a Class

In the syntax above, we have defined the cat object as Frisky by showing the dot operator to access the members of that object. This means that in order to assign 10 to the age of Frisky, you will need to write it out as frisky.itsAge=10. You will be able to do this the same way with all of the other parts that you need including the name, the display cat and so much more.

In the example above, you were able to access a lot of different variables from the class object. But this is not the most convenient way to go through and get all of the variables. There are other ways that you are able to do this by using the accessor method to provide information hiding or encapsulation to the syntax. A good example of this is below:

class Cat(object) itsAge

= None itsWeight

= None itsName

= None

#set accessor function use to assign values to the fields or member vars

def setItsAge(self, itsAge):

self.itsAge = itsAge

def setItsWeight(self, itsWeight):

self.itsWeight = itsWeight

def setItsName(self, itsName):

self.itsName =itsName

#get accessor function use to return the values from a field

def getItsAge(self):

return self.itsAge

def getItsWeight(self):

return self.itsWeight

def getItsName(self):

return self.itsName

```
objFrisky = Cat()

objFrisky.setItsAge(5)

objFrisky.setItsWeight(10)

objFrisky.setItsName("Frisky")

print("Cats Name is:", objFrisky.getItsname())

print("Its age is:", objFrisky.getItsAge())

print("Its weight is:", objFrisky.getItsName())
```

The output that you are going to get from all of this will be the following:

```
('Cats Name is:', 'Frisky')

(Its age is:', 5)

('Its weight is:', 10)
```

In the example above, you are using the accessor methods in order to set up and get the member variables. This is done often for data hiding or for encapsulation. Encapsulation is done if the variables are protected or private, but inside of the Python language, all of the member variables are going to be set to public by default.

For example, in this language, you are not going to find keywords like private, protected, and public in order to define their accessibility. So basically all of your attributes are going to be public.

Many languages that are like Python, such as other OOP languages, are going to prevent access to the attributes of different instances or classes, with the idea being that if the programmer of the class didn't define or set up a method to manipulate the attribute, then the user of this instance has no right to change it or even to examine it.

But Python is not going to use this approach. With the attribute reference syntax, you are able to access most of the instance and the class attributes, and when using the __dict__attribute, the entire thing can be shown.

If you are someone who has used C++ or Java in the past and you would like to use some of the programming techniques that will allow you to protect the variables and functions that you are making in Python, or at least make them private, it is possible. You will need to work on these a bit and make some changes, but it is possible to protect the work that you are doing in Python, even when Python assumes that everything is public.

What is the process of name mangling?

When you are using a compiler construction, the process of name mangling, or you may find it as name decoration, is a technique that allows you to solve different problems in the code that are caused by a need to resolve unique names for the programming entities in many of the more modern programming languages.

It is basically going to provide you with a way of encoding more information into the class, structure, function, and other datatype within the order to pass on more of the semantic information that you need from the compilers over to the linkers.

There are some times when the language will allow different entities to have the same identifier as a name, as long as they are going to take up different namespace. These namespaces are going to be defined by their explicit namespace, class, or module. They can also use the same identifier for a name if they have different signatures, such as a function overload.

Any object that is produced by a compiler is going to be linked with other pieces of the object code by a linker. The linker is going to need a lot of information about each of the entities within the program. For example, if you want to link a function, you will need the name of the function, the number of arguments that are inside, and so on so that the link is making sure to pick the right information.

In Python, you are able to do name mangling in your private class members. You are able to use this by giving them a name that will have two leading underscores and no more than one that is trailing. For example, saying __thing will work fine with this, but having __thing__ will not work.

Pythons runtime is not going to restrict access to the members, but the mangling is only going to prevent name collisions of a derived class defines a member with the same name.

When Python encounters name mangled attributes, it is going to transform these names with a single underscore and the name of the enclosing class. Python will be able to automatically change the name so that the references to this attribute, when made in the usual way, end up failing.

The main reason for using name mangling in Python here is to show that the program is going to take care of the class attributes and the name is mangled to help prevent a conflict with the program. It is also a way that Python makes sure that you are only using them in cases when you really need to, not just because you think that you should.

When you are using the name mangling, keep in mind that these underscores are not going to change the way that your method will be accessed. They are better off used for inheritances and other options so that you are able to build things like hierarchies without having to worry about a name collision.

The best strategy to do here is to get used to the model where all of the codes in a single process will be able to get along well without having to use any of these private options or worrying about name mangling since this is a complicated process that is sometimes difficult to handle in Python.

So the next question that you may have is if these underscores are really going to help you to make things private. Unfortunately, they are not going to work in the same way that you are used to when working in the other programming languages like C#, Java, and C++.

Everything in Python is going to be public so the best bet is to insist that the other collaborators read and follow the documentation that you have in place.

Property

A property gets and sets a value. It is going to work just like the methods do in Python, but the syntax is a bit easier to use. A property is often assigned like a variable and this causes the setter method to be executed. In the cat class that we used above, you have already used a getter and a setter in the properties. The setter property is going to assign a value to the member variables and the getter property will return a value from the member variables.

Instances and static methods

When you are using a static method, you will be able to call them out without having to create an object of a class using the new class names. This is because the static method will not accepting a self instance.

On the other hand, when you are using an instance method, you will be required to use an object of a class and have it created before it can be called. These two are opposite of each other and which one you use will depend on whether you want to create an object or not when you are working on the syntax.

Objects and classes are important parts of working with your syntaxes. The objects are going to be the part where you are able to define what you are using within the statement and you will be able to define them in the way that you would like.

The class is going to be the section that will contain all of the different options that you would like to define within the program. This section took some time to use the example of a cat, linking together all of the cat objects, such as age, name, and weight, into the same class. You are able to do so much when you get started with this and you can make your own classes based on the different things that you are working on with your particular program.

Take some time to try out a few of the different syntaxes and statements that we have inside of this chapter. This will help you to get some more practice with using your interpreter and seeing what all you are able to do with the Python program. You can mix around to use different scenarios when you get started and mix up how many of the variables you would like to use as well to make this more entertaining and to learn what all you are able to do with this kind of programming.

Chapter 8: What are Inheritances and How do They Work in Python?

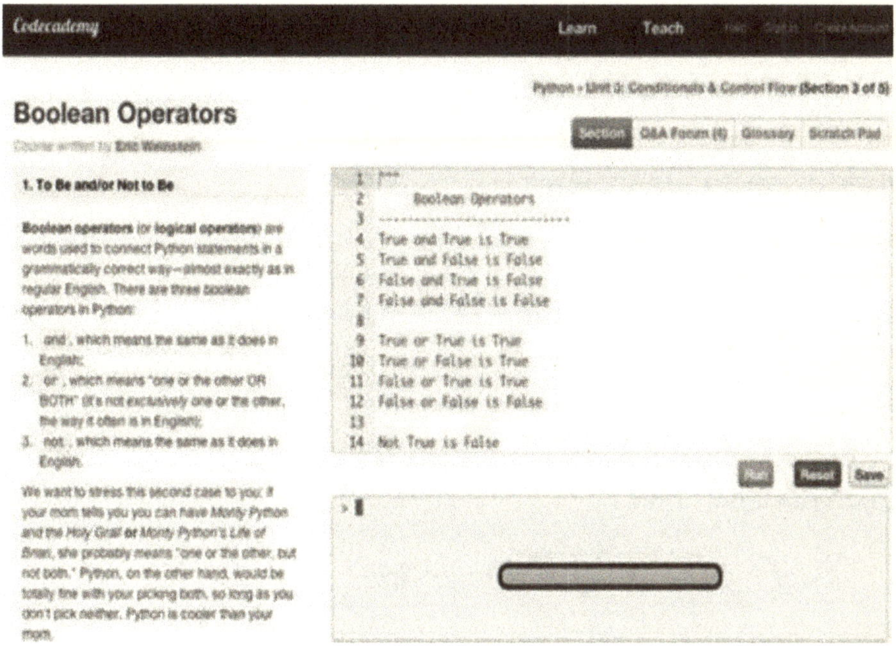

Inheritance is one of the main features that you will find in OOP, including in the python language, which will allow your user to create a derived class from an existing base class. The new derived class will inherit all of the features that were in a base class and you can add in some more features if you would like.

We took a look at this in some of the other chapters, but we will look a bit more and see how they will affect your code writing. Here is an example of what you may see when working on an inheritance.

```
#Example of inheritance
#base class
class Student(object):
        def__init__(self, name, rollno):
        self.name = name
        self.rollno = rollno
#Graduate class inherits or derived from Student class
class GraduateStudent(Student):
        def__init__(self, name, rollno, graduate):
        Student__init__(self, name, rollno)
        self.graduate = graduate

def DisplayGraduateStudent(self):
```

```
        print"Student Name:", self.name)

        print("Student Rollno:", self.rollno)

        print("Study Group:", self.graduate)


#Post Graduate class inherits from Student class

class PostGraduate(Student):

        def__init__(self, name, rollno, postgrad):

        Student__init__(self, name, rollno)

        self.postgrad = postgrad


        def DisplayPostGraduateStudent(self):

        print("Student Name:", self.name)

        print("Student Rollno:", self.rollno)

        print("Study Group:", self.postgrad)


#instantiate from Graduate and PostGraduate classes

        objGradStudent = GraduateStudent("Mainu", 1, "MS-
Mathematics")

        objPostGradStudent = PostGraduate("Shainu", 2,
"MS-CS")
```

objPostGradStudent.DisplayPostGraduateStudent()

When you type this into your interpreter, you are going to get the results:

('Student Name:', 'Mainu')

('Student Rollno:', 1)

('Student Group:', 'MSC-Mathematics')

('Student Name:', 'Shainu')

('Student Rollno:', 2)

('Student Group:', 'MSC-CS')

Overriding the Bass Class for Your Derived Class

There are some times when you are going to need to override the bass class in order to bring it into the derived class. The basic meaning of overriding in the OOP is basically replacing the same parental behavior so that it is present in the child class.

You can add these features to the child class and then add in or change some of the features to make them work the way that you would like. Through this method, the class is able to copy another class, while also avoiding duplicating the code, while also having the ability to customize or enhance part of the new code. This is why it is so important to learn how to do this so that you can make the exact code that you would like.

Overloading

Another thing that you are able to do when you work with your inheritance class is overloading. Overloading is basically the ability to use one single identifier in order to define more than one method inside of a class that differ in the input and the output parameters.

The overload methods are going to be used when they will execute the same task conceptually, but there will be small differences in the set parameters. Overloading will also allow you to define two ore more functions that have the same names but with different signatures, such as the number of parameters.

For the most part, you will not need to use the overload function. Python is a dynamically typed program and it is going to support optional arguments in the functions so the overloading process is not usually something you will need to worry about.

If you do decide to use the overloading process, you are going to have to download the write module to help you out with this. You will be able to install the module from https://github.com/bintoro/overloading.py

When you have had time to install the module and open it up from your command prompt or the command shell and type in the following information:

- $ Python overloading.py install in Windows or Linux

- Pip install overloading in Linux. If the pip is installed windows then you can also go with this command.
- Now import the module from the overloading import and then it should work as overloading for you.

While we have spent some time talking about overloading, it is important to note that the Python programming language is not going to use the overload function.

This is a dynamically typed language that will allow you to add in optional arguments to your functions so there really is no reason to need the overloading feature unless you are using one of the other programming languages with your code.

Method overloading

Inside of Python 3.4 there has been an additional feature added that allows for method overloads. This makes it easier to perform some different operations based on the type of your first argument.

When making a generic function, you are going to have one that is composed of multiple functions implementing the same operation for different types. Which type of implementation that you should use during this call is going to be determined by the dispatch algorithm. When the implementation is chosen based on the type of just one single argument, this is going to be known as a single dispatch.

To define a generic function, you will need to decorate it using the @singledispatch decorator. Note that the dispatch happens on the type of the first argument.

Operator Overloading

When you are working in operator overloading, it means that you are going to give more than one meaning to the standard operators, applying to object constructed fro programmer defined classes.

There are many different operators that you can use inside of your code including division signs, multiplication, subtraction, and addition signs.

But there are times when you are going to need to do an overloading function in order to ensure that the program is going to do what you would like.

For example, if you don't do the operator overloading on the formula, equations such as ¾ and 2/3 are not going to show up in the program in the way that you would like.

Multiple inheritance

Another feature that you can do inside of inheritance with Python is the multiple inheritance. This is a feature in which a class can inherit some methods and attribute from two or more parent classes. This means that ClassC is going to get some features from ClassB and then ClassB had gotten some of their features from ClassA.

Remember that doing a circular inheritance is not a possibility when working in Python, but you can use a few parent classes to help put together a new class in the code.

Working with inheritance inside of your codes can make things easier. It takes some of the features and methods that you are using inside one of your codes and allows you to put it into the new code and make changes and adjustments that you need to make something amazing.

You can even use a few different parent methods to make a new one if you would like to. There are just so many things that you are able to do when working with inheritance and you will be able to save a lot of time and effort when you are able to use inheritance in some of your codes.

Working in Python can be one of the best coding languages that you can use. There are so many things that you are able to do with your codes, from creating a simple code that will have a statement show up, creating loops that will have the same information come back up again and again, and so much more.

This guidebook is meant to help you out with learning some more that comes with Python after you have had some time to learn it before. These are nice codes that will help you out so much when working within the language and getting the more complex codes that you want. You need to have a bit of experience behind you to get started on this, but it is going to make things more fun when you can do some of these options.

We spent a lot of time working on the new topics including regular expressions, exception handling, and more. It will not take too long before you are able to add all of these things together and make some of the best code that you could ever imagine.

It does not matter if you have used code in the past or you are just getting started, you are going to find that Python is one of the best coding languages that you can use to make some powerful code. This guidebook is going to show you how to get started with some more complicated codes so that you can make some more of the programs that you have always wanted to accomplish.

Printed in September 2019
by Rotomail Italia S.p.A., Vignate (MI) - Italy